Old STEVENSTON

by
R. & M. McSherry

Brake Plough Stevenston.

M.177a.

The Break Plough was a small group of cottages situated at the north end of Stevenston near Kerelaw Mains Farm. It was better known locally as the Brackleheugh or the Brakplow and attracted many artists, who came to paint the peaceful dell.

© R. & M. McSherry 1998
First published in the United Kingdom, 1998,
by Stenlake Publishing, Ochiltree Sawmill, The Lade,
Ochiltree, Ayrshire, KA18 2NX
Telephone / Fax: 01290 423114
ISBN 1 84033 042 2

THE PUBLISHERS REGRET THAT THEY CANNOT SUPPLY
COPIES OF ANY PICTURES FEATURED IN THIS BOOK.

ACKNOWLEDGEMENTS

Thanks are due to the following, who provided information and/or pictures:
E. Clark; ex Provost James Clements; L. Cowan; J. Dodds; J. McColl;
J. McLelland; the North Ayrshire Museum; and M. Paterson

In July 1952, after nearly fifty years of petitioning, Stevenston was elevated to burgh status, and as a result required a coat of arms and motto. The Lord Lyon (Sir Thomas Innes of Learny at the time), who has the final word on heraldry in Scotland, did not approve of the final submissions. After a deputation from the council met him in Edinburgh an agreeable coat of arms and motto was accepted, depicting symbols associated with the town and its heritage. The arms show the black shakefork of Cunninghame on a silver field. The black diamond represents the town's associations with mining, and a stick of gelignite denotes the explosives that were produced at Ardeer. Stephen Loccard or Lockhart, from whom the town derives its name, is commemorated by the lock with a heart in the centre. Stevenston's motto comes from Robert Burns's ballad *Bonnie Lesley*, which he wrote in honour of Miss Lesley Baillie, daughter of Robert Baillie of Mayville, Stevenston.

INTRODUCTION

The parish of Stevenston derives its name from Stephen Loccard or Lockhart, whose father obtained a grant of land from Richard de Morville, Lord of Cunninghame and Constable of Scotland, *circa* 1170. It was later passed to the Loudon family and from them to the Cunninghames and the Earl of Glencairn. Glencairn was a great rival of the head of the Montgomeries, the Earl of Eglinton.

The power to dominate north Ayrshire caused a feud between the two families which lasted more than a century, causing the destruction of castles at Kerelaw and Eglinton estates and the death of many members of both families. In 1595 Eglinton and Glencairn were cited to appear before the King and Council at Holyrood House in Edinburgh to settle the long-standing feud. However, Glencairn failed to appear and was outlawed, although as time passed the policy of the government changed and the feud came to an end.

The Cunninghames developed Stevenston's coalfields, and in 1700 Robert Cunninghame built Saltcoats harbour, mainly for the export of coal to Ireland. He also built the salt pans where inferior quality coal was used in the manufacture of salt. The estate passed to Robert Reid Cunninghame, who in 1772 built a short canal, the first industrial canal in Scotland, from the coalfields to Saltcoats harbour. In 1774 Cunninghame developed a co-partnership in coal mining with Patrick Warner of Ardeer Estate who also had mines in the area.

Weaving was a cottage industry in Stevenston, and the area above the main street was known as Weavers' Brae. At a small hamlet called Pipersheugh on the outskirts of Stevenston Jew's harps were made. Heavy industry was important too and in 1849 Glengarnock Iron and Steel Company built an ironworks on the foreshore, which was operational for eighty years. Three iron foundries operated in the Ardeer area. Local quarries produced good quality stone known as Stevenston stone which was used in house-building and also exported to Ireland.

In 1871 the Swedish inventor and scientist, Alfred Nobel, visited Scotland and set up the British Dynamite Company (later Nobel's Explosive Company) at the Ardeer Sandhills. This proved to be an ideal location for manufacturing explosives, and the factory brought much prosperity to the area. It became the largest manufacturer of explosives in the world, dominating in research, development and export. Alfred Nobel, who died in 1896, was known as 'the richest vagabond in Europe', having never settled anywhere. He bequeathed funds for the establishment of the Nobel foundation which today funds annually awarded prizes for contributions to peace, physics, chemistry, physiology and medicine, literature and economics. In 1926 Nobel's Ardeer factory played an important part in the formation of Imperial Chemical Industries. Ardeer employed nearly 13,000 at its peak in the forties, but is now staffed by only two or three hundred people.

After petitions in 1904 and 1926, a 1952 campaign was successful in seeing Stevenston promoted to burgh status. One of the last towns in Scotland to achieve this, the formation of district and regional councils in 1974 saw the demise of the burgh.

What does the future hold for Stevenston after 800 years of existence? Part of the former Nobel plant has been designated as a new heritage centre for the millennium, and the town is looking forward to this era and endeavouring TO SPREAD HER CONQUESTS FURTHER.

Provost James Morrison admiring the new Stevenston Council chains of office in his home in June 1953. Provost Morrison was elected after polling top in the first town council elections in July 1952. He had long fought for burgh status. The provost's chain was presented by the Imperial Chemical Industries; Provost Morrison gifted the bailies' chains of office and also the robes for the three magistrates. He was 93 when elected and lived to the grand old age of 104.

An early photograph of the Cross, when an open burn still ran through it. The building behind the shop was originally a brewery which used water from the burn for its ale.

The Cross, with the brigs crossing the burn and the brewery building in the centre. In 1924, due to the increase in traffic and in an effort to create jobs, it was decided to remove the bridges and buildings and to tunnel the burn underground. The new wider road through the Cross was suitable for motorised vehicles.

Old Bridge and Townhead, Stevenston

Townhead, showing Warner's Brig before the area was transformed by road improvements in 1924. The age of the motor car was about to begin. H. McKechan's tailor and draper's shop is on the right.

An early street scene looking towards Townhead. The road surface is poor but at the time it was only used by horse-drawn vehicles. The area beyond the Brigs was once known as Weavers' Brae.

An early 1900s picture of New Street (Coo-rodden) with the gasworks on the extreme left. Stevenston Public School (right) opened in 1875 and is now the site of Glencairn Primary School. On the wall beyond the school playground is an advertisement for John Boyle, Bootmaker. The cottages on the left were demolished many years ago, and the buildings which replaced them have also been demolished and modern houses built on the site.

SCHOOL AND NEW STREET, STEVENSTON

D 1890

New Street leading to the Cross. Pupils attended the Stevenston Higher Grade Public School from primary to the third year of secondary education. Building work began when a new Education Act was passed in 1872; work was completed and the school was opened in 1875. The school was destroyed by fire in 1982 and replaced in 1984 by Glencairn Primary, all secondary education having previously moved to the new Auchenharvie Academy, which opened on 26 August 1971. On the left of the picture is the De Luxe cinema and Joseph Clark's pawnbroker's sign.

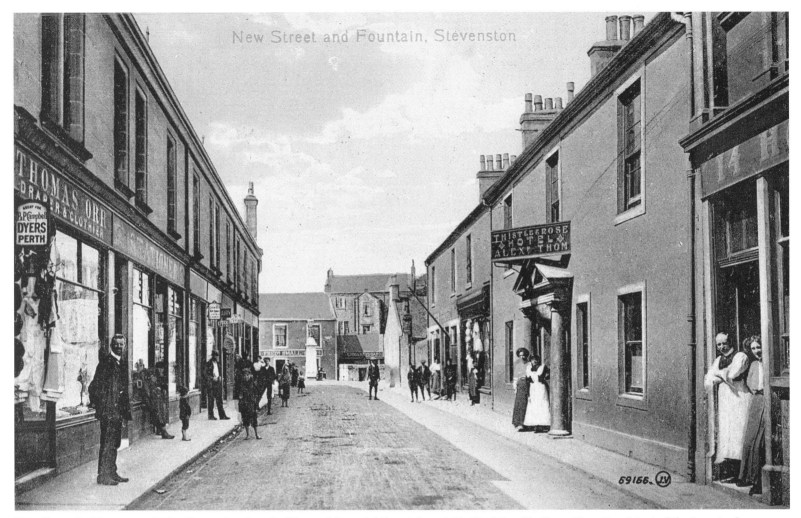

New Street looking towards the Cross, showing the Warner Memorial Fountain outside Fred Small's Cross Keys Bar. Most of the town's shops were situated in this area. On the right is the Thistle and Rose Hotel, where the 'Stivinstone' Masonic Lodge (Thistle and Rose) - No. 169 in the Grand Roll of Scotland - was founded in 1787. Meetings were initially held in premises in Schoolwell Brae and Weavers' Brae, and later in Warner's Ardeer house, but the Thistle and Rose Hotel became the lodge's meeting place from 1814 until a new temple was opened at 64 New Street in 1954.

New Street from North, Stevenston

The northern part of New Street, whose original name of Coo-rodden derived from the days when the road led to the town's common grazing ground. It looks as if a photocall has been arranged for all the shop owners and customers to pose for the photographer. The picture was taken in the early 1900s.

A 1910 view of Shore Road with Ardeer Church in the distance. On the left is Crawford's grocery store which later became Gilmours, and on the right hand corner Oswald the drapers with the gas lamp above the door.

The Parish Church of Stevenston, better known as the High Kirk, has a commanding view overlooking the town. A smaller church was built on the site in 1670 and as the population increased additions were made to it. Dr David Landsborough was minister from 1811 and had the old church demolished in 1832. The new church, above, was dedicated in 1833. Dr Lansborough continued to be the minister until the Disruption of 1843 when many left the Established Church and set up the Free Church. Repairs to the church spire and roof took place in the early 1990s.

Stevenston from the High Road

A 1920s view overlooking the town from the High Road, with the industrial buildings of Ardeer in the distance.

The High Road villas, built of Stevenston quarry stone at the end of the nineteenth century, were ideally located, being close to the town centre whilst having commanding views of the surrounding countryside. The opening to the left of the picture leads to Mayville House, once the home of Lesley Baillie, whose beauty was celebrated by Robert Burns in his poem *Bonnie Lesley*. The monument erected by Lesley Baillie's father in memory of his wife was re-erected on its present site in Glencairn Street and unveiled on 15 June 1929 when Bonnie Lesley's name was added to it. It is now a public monument maintained by the local council.

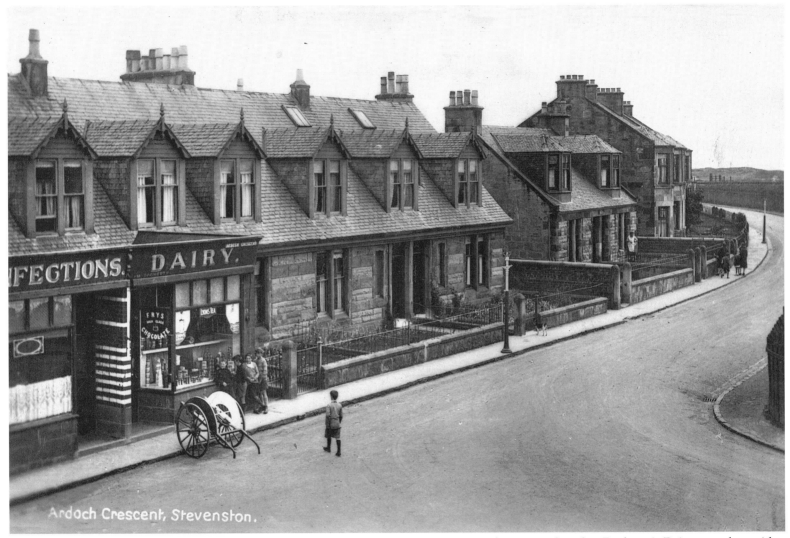

Ardoch Crescent, Stevenston.

Ardoch Crescent, photographed in the 1920s. There are two shops in the picture, one a confectioners, the other Docherty's Dairy, complete with a handbarrow for deliveries outside.

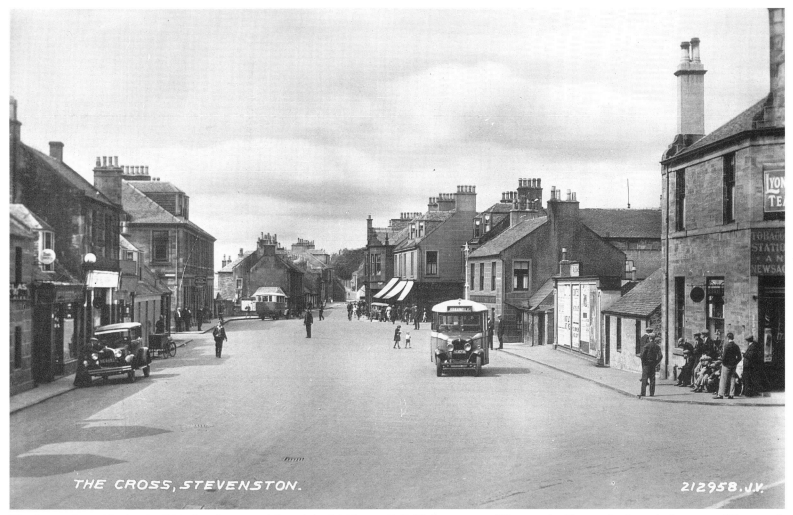

THE CROSS, STEVENSTON.

212958. J.V.

The Cross after widening in 1924, showing one of the original A1 buses (AG 4714) *en route* to Kilmarnock. The service from Ardrossan to Kilmarnock commenced in January 1926 and continued until the owners of A1 sold out to Stagecoach on 30 January 1995.

Bridge,& Fountain, Stevenston.

The Jubilee Bridge, spanning the Stevenston Burn, and the drinking fountain in the background, were both erected to commemorate Queen Victoria's Golden Jubilee (1887). Records show that the burn had an abundant supply of salmon and trout, salmon being the staple diet of many of the underprivileged in Stevenston at the beginning of the nineteenth century.

Following the collapse of pipes installed to carry the Stevenston Burn under the roadway, the Cross area was closed in January 1982 while the underground channel was repaired and reinforced.

Stevenston's original station, built by the Glasgow and South Western Railway, also included the station-master's house. At one time the footbridge was heavily used because of the number of times the level crossing had to be closed. This was due to the large number of freight trains travelling to the coal pits, iron foundries and to Nobel's explosives factory, not to mention the frequent passenger services from Largs to Glasgow and Ardrossan to Kilmarnock. The level crossing is still a hindrance to traffic after 150 years in operation.

This scene of drovers resting their animals beside the burn at the Cross was a common one prior to the turn of the century. Many of the animals were shipped to Ardrossan from Dublin or Belfast, and were then herded to the market in Kilwinning, with private deals being frequently made *en route*. Animals belonging to people in New Street, then better known as the Coo-rodden or Cow Street, were also grazed on this piece of common ground.

The Hayocks area was a mid-1930s housing development, built to provide homes for the increasing number of ICI workers. Many were transferred from other works to the new plants that were developed at Ardeer, in particular the detonator and blackpowder plants. On the left of the picture is the old Blue Star Garage with a sign pointing to Largs. The shop on the right was known locally as 'Pop's'.

When Robert Cunninghame had to dispose of part of his estate, Ardeer was sold to the Rev. Patrick Warner of Irvine on his retiral from the ministry in 1709. He continued to live there until his death in 1724. In 1926 the Warner trustees put the house and grounds on the market and in 1928 it was purchased by Stevenston Parish Council. A year later they resold it to Nobel's Explosive Company Ltd for the same price that they had purchased it for, £5,000. The house was renamed Ardeer Recreation Club and was used for many purposes by employees of Nobel's. There was a large hall mainly used for dancing, and indoor sports facilities included billiard and snooker rooms, badminton, table tennis, boxing and rifle shooting. There was a football stadium with an athletic track, plus tennis courts, rugby and hockey fields, bowling greens and a cricket field. Ardeer was also the headquarters of the Ardeer Cadet Force. The main house was demolished in 1961 and a modern clubhouse built in its place. With the declining number of personnel at Ardeer Factory, however, and changing trends in entertainment and sport, it was closed. The house was subsequently bought and an attempt was made to continue it as a club, although this was unsuccessful and the building was demolished in 1992. All that remains today is the indoor shooting range, the bowling green and the football field.

Hayocks House was built in the early 1800s by a relative of the Cunninghames of Auchenharvie and Kerelaw. It was later renamed Ardchoille House by Mr McGregor of Ardeer Foundry, and in the late 1940s became a hotel. The ground in front of the building was converted into a football field, the home of Ardeer Thistle Football Club from 1952 until 1973. This match was played during the 1959 season, a very successful one which saw the club win many of the county trophies. They played forty matches undefeated until the replay against Greenock in the Scottish Cup semi-final. Tommy Duffy created a record by scoring 96 goals during the season. The team were well supported, as can be seen from this photograph.

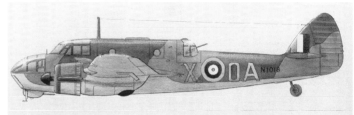

Flying Officer Kenneth Campbell VC was the youngest son of James Campbell of Kerelaw House (above). He became a pilot while studying at Cambridge, and received his commission as a pilot officer in 1939 in the RAF Volunteer Reserve. He lost his life when piloting a Beaufort Torpedo Bomber and attacking the German battleship *Gneisenua* at mast height in Brest Harbour on 6 April 1941. Evidence for the citation was provided by the French Underground and on 10 March 1942 he was posthumously awarded the Victoria Cross for conspicuous bravery. He was the first RAFVR member to be awarded the VC. Today one of the VC10 Aircraft of No. 10 Squadron, No. XR 808, is named Kenneth Campbell VC.

Kerelaw has a long association with the history of Ayrshire. In the twelfth century the estate was the home of the Loccard family, one of whom, Stephen, gave his name to Stevenston. It subsequently passed to members of the Cunninghame family, and during their feud with the Montgomeries was plundered in 1488. Forty years later the Cunninghames burned down Eglinton Castle in revenge. In 1685 Kerelaw was owned by John Hamilton of Grange, near Kilmarnock. His great-grandson became a general in the American War of Independence and is reputed to have drafted the Declaration of Independence. A modern mansion house was built by Alexander Hamilton in 1778, and later sold to Gavin Fullerton, a West Indian merchant. In 1919 it was purchased by James Campbell WS, who was the town clerk of Saltcoats. His was the last family to live at Kerelaw, and in 1969 it was purchased by Glasgow Corporation Education Department who built a List D school within its grounds. This opened on 22 June 1970. Kerelaw House, which was built in the Adam style, was to be used as a staff and administrative centre for the school. It was bulldozed to the ground, allegedly by accident.

1st Stevenston Boys Brigade company, one of Ayrshire's oldest, was officially registered at BB Headquarters on 23 September 1892. The company has adapted to the numerous changes that have taken place in the organisation over the last 100 years, and the BBs are still well supported today. The photograph was taken at the BB centenary celebrations held in 1983.

Secondary 1AB class at the Higher Grade School, photographed in 1956.

The Ardeer Thistle team of 1924-25. This was one of the club's great seasons, and it won all the junior trophies it competed in with the exception of the Scottish Cup. Team members are, left to right, standing: Strang; James Crapnell; McQueen; A. Taylor; Wilson; Joe Crapnell. Sitting: R. Mackie; B. Conn; J. Bryant; J. Curley; J. Lindsay; A. McWhinney (trainer). In the following season the final of the Ayrshire Cup was played at Rugby Park, Kilmarnock. Due to the National Strike no transport was available, and instead a march to the game was organised, led by the Stevenston Temperance Pipe Band. Ardeer Thistle triumphed and returned with the cup. Due to lack of funds the club closed down two years later, but was restarted in 1952 thanks mainly to the efforts of Mr R. Paterson (newsagent) and Councillor J. Clements. Today Ardeer Thistle play in the Stagecoach Western League at the old Ardeer Recreation Club field.

Ardeer Recreation Club had the only Rugby team in Stevenston, and this had a short career from early 1930 to 1950. Part of the town's municipal housing stock now stands on the rugby field. During the building of the houses a deep mining pit was discovered which had not been recorded on maps or plans of the area. The team is the 1946 XV. Left to right, back row: G. Khonstain; A. Wright; N. Picton; F. Nichol; D. McGhee; C.W. Crooks; J.S. Robertson; T. Jones. Front row: A. Cameron (captain); R. McSherry; A. McGregor; W.G. Lang; A. Mackenzie; P. Hughes; D. Vallance. There were no matching socks or shorts - the jerseys were normally red, but during the war the team played in a mixture of jerseys and it was not unusual for them all to be different.

W.&R. Halbert at the Cross were the town's transport pioneers. The bicycles on show in the windows would do any museum proud today. Many will remember the single petrol pump that trailed above the pavement to fuel motor vehicles. The shop and garage were demolished in the 1970s when the area was cleared in the Stevenston Comprehensive Development plan.

Inset: The interior of Halbert's Garage. Prior to the First World War Halbert's advertised in the *Stevenston Press and Saltcoats Advertiser*, which also included Christie's railway guide. The adverts described the fine selection of cycles they sold and repaired; go-carts and prams were re-tyred and wringers were re-covered too. They also sold a variety of accessories including sewing machine needles, paints and varnishes.

One of Morrisons horse-drawn bakery vans from the bakery at Fullerton Square on its daily rounds.

One of the early locomotives used for transporting coal from Stevenston coal pits to Ardrossan Harbour. The line opened in 1831 and was originally horse-drawn, but by 1840 Ardrossan Railway had purchased its first steam engine, a Bury model built by Barr & McNab of Paisley and named *Firefly*. It had a 2-4-0 wheel arrangement and a net weight of eight tons.

These ruins are often mistaken for an ancient keep, but are part of an early engine house which is now a listed building. It was built in 1719 in conjunction with the development of the Stevenston coalfield, and housed a Newcomen steam beam engine, employed principally to keep the coal workings at Auchenharvie No. 2 pit free of water. This was only the second such engine to be built in Scotland, and was not very efficient. The ruins of the engine house stand on Auchenharvie Golf Course.

Pit shaft sinkers at Auchenharvie at the turn of the century. This was a hard and dangerous job where special clothing was a must. The worker third from the right was John Robinson who emigrated to the USA and was killed in a mining accident.

Coal mining at Stevenston encouraged development, and as early as 1849 Glengarnock Iron Company built five blast furnaces on the foreshore to smelt pig-iron. At the time iron ore was plentiful in the district, particularly in the Dalry area; ore was also imported from North Africa. Merry and Cunninghame succeeded the Glengarnock Company, employing around 1,000 at the works, operating round the clock in eight hour shifts. The depression years forced Merry & Cunninghame into liquidation in 1931 and the works were demolished in 1935, ending another industrial chapter in the town's history.

The Daylight Mine at Auchenharvie, which used an endless haulage system to bring coal from the five pits up the ramp in the centre of the picture. The last of the Stevenston mines to close was the Bumbee Pit where production stopped in 1926. The Nylon works were later built on this site.

Left: This picture is believed to show one of the six Auchenharvie pits, the last of which closed in 1915. Tragedy occurred on 2 August 1895 when water burst into No. 4 mine, trapping fourteen men. It took almost two days to reach the men, only five of whom survived. A memorial cairn was erected 98 years later at the side of the putting green at Auchenharvie Golf Club, in line with the original workings where the miners were lost.

The entrance to Nobel's factory at the turn of the century. At its peak the factory employed 12,700 people, and for over 125 years this was where they arrived for work. The entrance was recently moved a further 400 metres inside the premises, which now employ a work-force of only a few hundred. The manager's house is on the right, with the main office and clock tower in the centre. Known locally as 'the factory', it once sustained the economies of the Three Towns and Kilwinning, and its slow demise has had a disastrous effect.

The original office block and clock tower at Nobel's. Managerial staff occupied the lower floor in the main building, which was demolished in 1975.

An early aerial photograph of the Ardeer Sandhills showing the blasting huts surrounded by mounds of sand for safety.

Although run jointly by the G&SWR and Caledonian Railways at the turn of the century, this station and the line leading to it was referred to as Nobel's private line. This picture shows prime ministers from the colonies accompanied by their guests and the provost and magistrates of the City of Glasgow. They had all previously attended the Coronation of King Edward VII, and their visit was an unusual event as guests were not encouraged to visit the factory in large numbers. The special rail carriages were loaned for the occasion by the Caledonian Railway Company. Built in 1896 with a platform long enough to accommodate two trains, Ardeer was one of the busiest stations in the district and was used solely by the employees of the factory. During the 1940s, when production was at its highest, a second rail platform was used at the Garnock site. Ardeer Station closed in 1966.

Construction of the Ardeer Nylon Works commenced in 1966, but the plant was not operational until 1969. The two chimneys were 400 feet high and the concrete cooling tower measured 375 feet; it was a considerable landmark in the area until it collapsed in strong winds six years after being constructed. The works, which employed 1,100 people at one stage, had a very short life, closing in 1981 after only 12 years of operation. The nitric acid plant that also occupied the site was incorporated into the works at Ardeer but only survived a few years. The site of the nylon works has now been developed into a business park.

A distance of twenty miles of main railway was developed inside the Ardeer factory, and in addition to this a total of seventy-five miles of bogey railways ran to all points of the compass within the site. Diesel 'dinkies' were used for pulling heavy loads. During the war women were co-opted to take over many of the jobs previously done by men, and this picture shows the first women dinky driver and her crew member. Note the victory signs on the side of the bogies.

A delegation of Chinese and Japanese VIPs on a grand tour of Ardeer Factory in 1900. The improvised transport must have caused a few wry comments from the work-force of the day.

Searchers were a familiar sight at entrances to all Nobel factory danger areas. They were responsible for ensuring that no banned items (such as metal objects, which could create a spark) passed beyond their box or gate.

The clubhouse of Ardeer Golf Club, on the eighteen hole course built in 1901 at the Misk Knowes. The club's original nine hole course was built on the foreshore in 1880; the second course had to make way for the ICI Nylon Plant in 1966. Ardeer then moved up country to Greenhead and built a fine course with spectacular views and a stamina-sapping 16th hole. The club has associations with many outstanding golfers - Jamie Anderson won the Open Championship in 1877, 1878 and 1879, W. Ferrie in 1883. Hamilton McInally, the outstanding Ayrshire amateur, was Scottish Champion in 1937, 1938 and 1947. Stevenston now also has a nine hole municipal course plus a driving range, operated by North Ayrshire Council. It was built over the original coal mining area and the infill of the 'White Lady', the name given to the previously flooded area at Auchenharvie.

Brown's Merrymakers Dance Band was synonymous with the Ardeer Recreation Club, and played to dancers of different generations from the early 1930s to the final session in August 1964. Three of the original quartet, Tom, David and George Brown, were present until the end. The fourth member, Eddie Cowan, had been killed in a motor cycle accident but his son, trumpeter Logan Cowan, played with the band. Outwith the 'Rec' the band was popular at formal dances during its long-playing career.

The bakers at Park Brothers pose in front of the company van with driver Johnny Robertson in the early 1920s. James Tait, on the right, arrived from Kirriemuir to work for the summer of 1919 and stayed with the bakery for a further forty-three years. On his left are the three Park brothers, Dick, Bob and Alex. The main bakery was in Main Street but they also had a shop in Warner Street, which was famous for its morning rolls.

A ploughman with a fine pair of Clydesdale horses at Kerelaw Farm. This was a familiar sight on farms in the earlier part of this century before the tractor took over.

Many of Stevenston's local farms disappeared to make way for industry, and, in the 1930s, for housing developments. This 1920s picture shows corn stooks being loaded onto a cart at Kerelaw Farm.